READING SYSTEM

STUDENT WORKBOOK SIX B

THIRD EDITION

by Barbara A. Wilson

Wilson Language Training
175 West Main Street
Millbury, Massachusetts 01527-1441
(508) 865-5699

ISBN 1-56778-099-7   Student Workbook Six B   Item# SW6B

The Wilson Reading System is published by:

Wilson Language Training Corp.
175 West Main Street
Millbury, MA 01527-1441

Printed in the U.S.A.

Read each suffix below.

en	ness	ful
ment	ly	er
ish	ive	ty
est	es	less
able	y	ing

Copy the suffix endings from above into the correct columns.

vowel suffixes   consonant suffixes

_____	_____		_____
_____	_____		_____
_____	_____		_____
_____	_____		_____
	_____		_____
			_____

Read the baseword. Select a suffix from the box at the top of the column to add to the baseword. Write the suffix and then the word on the lines provided.

ish	ing	er
est	y	es

ment	ness	ful
less	ly	ty

baby - _____ = _____

box - _____ = _____

wild - _____ = _____

dress - _____ = _____

gruff - _____ = _____

class - _____ = _____

shoplift - _____ = _____

publish - _____ = _____

thrill - _____ = _____

finish - _____ = _____

gloss - _____ = _____

mild - _____ = _____

child - _____ = _____

fast - _____ = _____

luck - _____ = _____

hope - _____ = _____

equip - _____ = _____

safe - _____ = _____

respect - _____ = _____

fist - _____ = _____

like - _____ = _____

distinct - _____ = _____

require - _____ = _____

tire - _____ = _____

use - _____ = _____

fond - _____ = _____

nine - _____ = _____

amuse - _____ = _____

bold - _____ = _____

neglect - _____ = _____

Write a suffix from the top of each box on the line to form a word.

ty ly ment	ive ment able	ly ty y
enrich_____	instinct_____	spunk____
consistent_____	depend_____	rude____
seven_____	command_____	safe____

ful er y	ing ful ness	es ing er
thrill____	defrost____	expand____
regret____	plump____	brush____
crisp____	trust____	thrill____

Write the words above on the lines below. Read the words.

_____   _____   _____

_____   _____   _____

_____   _____   _____

_____   _____   _____

_____   _____   _____

Underline or "scoop" the syllables in the baseword and circle the suffix in each word below.
Read the words.

brushes	preventive	dresser
candidly	crispy	thankless
embankment	blissful	stiffen
shyly	trusting	lameness
shadeless	thankless	blemishing
invested	spunky	classy
remotely	refresher	prideful
impurely	enrichment	amazement
zinger	stupidly	destructive
resulting	wildest	swelling
detachment	novelty	abolishment
refundable	plumpness	publishing
mildest	expandable	costly
lonely	crunches	regretful

List the words with vowel suffixes from previous page.

vowel suffixes

_____

_____

_____

_____

_____

_____

_____

_____

_____

_____

_____

_____

_____

_____

_____

_____

_____

List the words with consonant suffixes from previous page.

consonant suffixes

_____

_____

_____

_____

_____

_____

_____

_____

_____

_____

_____

_____

_____

_____

_____

_____

_____

Read the sentence. Select the correct word from the box to complete the sentence.
Write the word on the line. Reread the completed sentence. Use each word in the box only once.

expandable	hopeless	shipment	strongly
retirement	classy	lonely	difficulty
sulky	investment	destructive	kindly

1. Bob has had so much _____ with his Spanish class!

2. It is _____ ; we will not make the plane on time.

3. The wild fire was _____ to the homes.

4. Gramps is quite _____ *without* his wife.

5. I _____ hope for a happy ending to this novel!

6. The company made a costly _____ to Rome.

7. The man _____ gave his jacket to the cold child.

8. Pete's _____ from his company will be in June when he is sixty-five *years* old.

9. James will dress in a _____ tuxedo to attend the banquet.

10. That small ranch home is on an _____ lot.

11. Jed was _____ when his dad told him that he had to help with the dishes.

12. Mrs. Strom went to Cleveland to check on the _____ plan.

Underline or "scoop" the syllables in the baseword and circle the suffix. Write the two parts on the lines provided.

	Baseword	Suffix		Baseword	Suffix
thankful	=_____	- _____	dependable	=_____	- _____
publisher	=_____	- _____	mildest	=_____	- _____
frequently	=_____	- _____	slyly	=_____	- _____
selfish	=_____	- _____	freshen	=_____	- _____
longest	=_____	- _____	destructive	=_____	- _____
tireless	=_____	- _____	amazement	=_____	- _____
momently	=_____	- _____	silently	=_____	- _____
kindness	=_____	- _____	expanding	=_____	- _____
strongly	=_____	- _____	crunchy	=_____	- _____
statement	=_____	- _____	shoplifter	=_____	- _____
wildest	=_____	- _____	gruffest	=_____	- _____
refresher	=_____	- _____	boldly	=_____	- _____
blemishes	=_____	- _____	enrichment	=_____	- _____
regretful	=_____	- _____	investment	=_____	- _____
rudely	=_____	- _____	expandable	=_____	- _____

Write as many suffixes from memory as possible into the correct columns. Then, use your Rules Notebook to fill in any suffixes.

vowel suffixes   consonant suffixes

_____ _____   _____

_____ _____   _____

_____ _____   _____

_____ _____   _____

_____ _____   _____

_____

Use each word below in a sentence on the lines provided.

1. thankful

_____

2. lately

_____

3. equipment

_____

4. strongest

_____

5. wishing

_____

Read each sentence. Find the words with the -ed suffix in the sentences below. Underline the basewords and circle the suffixes in the -ed words.

1. The detective suspected the kid on the bench.

2. The students erupted when the substitute left the class.

3. Kevin predicted that Jenny *would* win.

4. Sandra protested the costly tax at the rally.

5. Fred insulted his pal by mistake.

Read each sentence above. Cover it and write the sentence below. Uncover it and proofread.

1. _____

_____

2. _____

_____

3. _____

_____

4. _____

_____

5. _____

_____

The -ed suffixes in the words above say /_____ /.

Proofread the sentences below. The underlined words are misspelled. Rewrite the sentence correctly on the lines provided adding capital letters and punctuation.

1. the <u>truk</u> stalled in five o'clock <u>traffik</u>

_____

2. these <u>thingz</u> belonged to mr fresno

_____

3. the <u>dentis</u> drilled my cavity

_____

4. the company <u>billd</u> me for the consultant

_____

5. i recalled the thrilling <u>amusemet</u> ride

_____

6. dad <u>filmd</u> the big event on video

_____

7. we must hire <u>skiled</u> *people* to get the job done

_____

8. what is this <u>nifte</u> thing called

_____

9. has the mold <u>jelld</u> yet

_____

10. the <u>comik</u> consistently thrilled his <u>fanz</u>

_____

The -<u>ed</u> suffixes in the words above say / _____ / .

Read each sentence. Find the words with the -ed suffix. Underline the baseword and circle the suffix.

1. Dave published his script and then made many sales.

2. Dad still wished to try the clams.

3. Sally wished that the game ended more quickly.

4. Steve brushed the dogs *after their* bath.

5. The debate was enriched by the tireless candidates.

6. Edna jumped in the van and it sped *away.*

7. The angry protester clenched her fist.

8. I expressed my disgust with a yell.

9. The kids were punished for missing class.

10. Tom finished the milkshake and then jumped in the lake.

The -ed suffixes in the words above say /_____/.

Underline the baseword and circle the suffix in each word below. Read the word.
Write /t/, /d/, or /ed/ above the suffix to indicate the sound.

filled	belonged	objected
restricted	blemished	bonked
responded	willed	stamped
happened	requested	expressed
consisted	thrilled	neglected
handcuffed	prolonged	impressed
distracted	clenched	complimented
called	trashed	demolished
infested	crunched	depended
erupted	suspected	killed
defended	winked	instilled
banged	resulted	convicted
recalled	fluffed	famished
rejected	camped	impacted

Read the sentence. Select the correct word from the box to complete the sentence.
Write the word on the line. Reread the completed sentence. Use each word in the box only once.

camped	jumped	expected	brushed
finished	insisted	longed	skilled
thrilled	winked	stressed	disrupted

1. Beth _____ for a ride Tom's hotrod.

2. The _____ man made a cabinet to hold the TV and VCR.

3. Gabe _____ the job and then went to the basketball game.

4. Dad _____ at Mom to tell her the plan was all set.

5. Kwon _____ to study his math *after* the big contest.

6. Jeff _____ off the cliff to go hang-*gliding*.

7. Kendra _____ her dad to ask him *about* the lunch plan.

8. I am _____ with the progress made by the students.

9. Jane felt _____ *about* the spelling quiz.

10. Peggy _____ that she did not mind helping at the event.

11. Cathy _____ time off to take care of Mike.

12. The kids _____ by the lake.

Add the suffix to each baseword. Above the ed , indicate the sound: /ed/, /d/, /t/.

happen	- ed = _____	insult	- ed = _____

happen   - ed = _____   insult   - ed = _____

thrill   - ed = _____   belong   - ed = _____

cross   - ed = _____   smell   - ed = _____

expect   - ed = _____   drench   - ed = _____

connect - ed = _____   stash   - ed = _____

defrost   - ed = _____   detect   - ed = _____

establish - ed = _____   bang   - ed = _____

risk   - ed = _____   dump   - ed = _____

chomp   - ed = _____   skill   - ed = _____

predict   - ed = _____   openmind - ed = _____

disrupt   - ed = _____   spell   - ed = _____

film   - ed = _____   punish   - ed = _____

longed   - ed = _____   stamp   - ed = _____

honk   - ed = _____   prevent   - ed = _____

host   - ed = _____   dull   - ed = _____

Copy the words from the previous page into the correct columns below.

-<u>ed</u> = /ed/   -<u>ed</u> = /d/   -<u>ed</u> = /t/

_____   _____   _____

_____   _____   _____

_____   _____   _____

_____   _____   _____

_____   _____   _____

_____   _____   _____

_____   _____   _____

_____   _____   _____

_____   _____   _____

Select one word from each group above to use in a sentence. Write the sentences below.

1. _____

   _____

2. _____

   _____

3. _____

   _____

Find all the suffixes in the sentences below. Underline the basewords and circle the suffixes.

1. Jane complimented Billy on his wise investment.

2. Sandy brushed the lint off her classy dress.

3. Ed swished the ball into the net in the basketball thriller.

4. Jim frequently stashed his cash in secret spots.

5. Sonya quickly mended the glossy costume.

Read each sentence above. Cover it and write the sentence below. Uncover it and proofread.

1. _____

_____

2. _____

_____

3. _____

_____

4. _____

_____

5. _____

_____

Combine the basewords and suffixes into words and write them on the lines. Read the words.

regret - ful - ly   =_____   fresh - en - ed   =_____

construct - ive - ly =_____   fret - ful - ly   =_____

grate - ful - ly   =_____   instinct - ive - ly =_____

effect - ive - ly   =_____   rest - ful - ly   =_____

care - less - ly   =_____   destruct - ive - ly =_____

thank - ful - ly   =_____   hate - ful - ly   =_____

use - ful - ly   =_____   impress - ive - ly =_____

trust - ful - ly   =_____   respect - ful - ly =_____

end - less - ly   =_____   care - less - ness =_____

hope - less - ly   =_____   help - ful - ly   =_____

will - ing - ness   =_____   sin - ful - ness   =_____

tact - ful - ly   =_____   protect - ive - ly =_____

life - less - ly   =_____   spite - ful - ness =_____

zest - ful - ly   =_____   use - less - ly   =_____

distinct - ive - ly =_____   zest - less - ly   =_____

Write a suffix from the top of each box on the line to form a word.

less ly ive	ive less ly	ly ful ive
use_____	care_____ness	wish____ly
object_____	thankful_____	disrespectful____
trustful_____	impress_____ly	select____ly

ful ive ly	ness ful ive	ful less ly
respect____ly	helpful____	tire____ly
effective____	tact____ly	fret____ly
protect____	instinct____ly	endless____

Write the words above on the lines below. Read the words.

_____ _____ _____

_____ _____ _____

_____ _____ _____

_____ _____ _____

_____ _____ _____

Read the words. Write the baseword and suffixes on the lines.

pridefully   =_____ _____ _____

tactfully   =_____ _____ _____

reflectively =_____ _____ _____

uselessly   =_____ _____ _____

skillfully   =_____ _____ _____

lifelessly   =_____ _____ _____

endlessly   =_____ _____ _____

hatefully   =_____ _____ _____

restlessness =_____ _____ _____

impressively =_____ _____ _____

inventiveness =_____ _____ _____

destructively =_____ _____ _____

respectfully =_____ _____ _____

neglectfully =_____ _____ _____

spitefulness =_____ _____ _____

carelessly   =_____ _____ _____

protectively =_____ _____ _____

restfully   =_____ _____ _____

hopefully   =_____ _____ _____

willingness   =_____ _____ _____

tactlessly   =_____ _____ _____

mindfully   =_____ _____ _____

tirelessly   =_____ _____ _____

zestfully   =_____ _____ _____

instinctively =_____ _____ _____

regretfully   =_____ _____ _____

constructively=_____ _____ _____

attractiveness=_____ _____ _____

effectively   =_____ _____ _____

zestlessly   =_____ _____ _____

Read the story "Tom Travels the Land" in Student Reader Six. Try to remember the sequence of events in the story and number the sentences below. Use the student reader to check your answers.

Tom Travels the Land

_____ Tom instinctively went to a soda shop in Texas.

_____ Tom finished high school and wished to travel across the U.S.A.

_____ Tom drove a van to Texas in five days.

_____ Tom had collected the cash to complete his trip across the entire U.S.A.

_____ Tom got a job in a soda shop in Atlanta.

Write the sentences above in the correct order on the lines below.

1. _____

_____

2. _____

_____

3. _____

_____

4. _____

_____

5. _____

_____

Underline or "scoop" the syllables in the baseword. Circle (separately) the two suffixes in each word.

blissfully	lifelessly	trustfully
uselessly	wishfully	willingness
impressively	hopefully	constructively
protectively	regretfully	respectfully
expectingly	helpfully	restfully
endlessly	attractively	collectively
tactfully	willingly	zestfully
sinfulness	carelessly	skillfully
helpfulness	gratefully	usefulness
wishfulness	distinctively	restlessly
thankfully	fatefully	selectively
spitefulness	thanklessness	carelessness
mindfully	carefully	sinfully
effectively	hopefully	effectiveness
actively	objectively	disrespectfully

Select a suffix from the first box and the second box to add to each baseword to form a word.
Write the whole word with suffixes on the lines provided.

Baseword - 1st suffix   - 2nd suffix

ive	ing
less	ful

ness
ly

help - _____ - _____ = _____

construct - _____ - _____ = _____

thank - _____ - _____ = _____

rest - _____ - _____ = _____

trust - _____ - _____ = _____

care - _____ - _____ = _____

will - _____ - _____ = _____

wish - _____ - _____ = _____

destruct - _____ - _____ = _____

effect - _____ - _____ = _____

use - _____ - _____ = _____

tire - _____ - _____ = _____

instinct - _____ - _____ = _____

zest - _____ - _____ = _____

act - _____ - _____ = _____

Find all the words with suffixes. Some will have one suffix; others will have two. Underline the baseword and circle the suffix(es). If there is more than one suffix, circle each suffix separately.

1. Rob willingly went to complete the task requirement.

2. Ed and Babs tirelessly constructed their *new* home.

3. Seth regretfully told Jan that he could not make the eventful date.

4. Teddy went in to take a nap, but he tossed restlessly in the bed.

5. Mom expressively thanked the kids for their helpfulness.

6. Tom carelessly spilled his plateful of chicken wings.

7. Neglectfully, Randy did not defrost the ham.

8. Betsy awoke and gratefully thanked her husband for doing the dishes.

9. Hopefully, crunchy candy is still in the dish.

10. Peg established a plan and zestfully began the job.

Write all the words with suffixes on the lines below.

1. _____ _____

2. _____ _____

3. _____ _____

4. _____ _____

5. _____ _____ _____ _____

6. _____ _____ _____ _____

7. _____

8. _____ _____ _____ _____

9. _____ _____

10. _____ _____

Read the words. Write the syllables on the lines. Mark the syllables. Mark the vowels.
e.g. <u>bū</u> <u>gle</u>
   o   cle

muffle = _____ _____   mantle = _____ _____

bugle = _____ _____   temple = _____ _____

grizzle = _____ _____   scuffle = _____ _____

sample = _____ _____   staple = _____ _____

duffle = _____ _____   mumble = _____ _____

puzzle = _____ _____   gamble = _____ _____

trifle = _____ _____   idle = _____ _____

thimble = _____ _____   fable = _____ _____

quibble = _____ _____   gable = _____ _____

ramble = _____ _____   cradle = _____ _____

humble = _____ _____   swizzle = _____ _____

cable = _____ _____   razzle = _____ _____

baffle = _____ _____   ladle = _____ _____

Bible = _____ _____   cattle = _____ _____

stifle = _____ _____   maple = _____ _____

battle = _____ _____   struggle = _____ _____

babble = _____ _____   bramble = _____ _____

haggle = _____ _____   able = _____ _____

brittle = _____ _____   noble = _____ _____

bottle = _____ _____   title = _____ _____

Read the sentences. Find the words with a consonant-le syllable.
Circle them and then divide the words by underlining or "scooping" each syllable.

1. those kids quibble over the smallest things

2. could you possibly staple these documents and then file them

3. the sample should effectively get us sales

4. i recommend this plan so that we can win the battle with that company

5. will the temple be constructed in the middle of the square

---

Rewrite each sentence adding capital letters and punctuation.

1. _____

   _____

2. _____

   _____

3. _____

   _____

4. _____

   _____

5. _____

   _____

Underline the syllables in the nonsense words below. Mark the syllable types (c =closed, o =open, c-le = consonant - le). Mark the vowels and read the nonsense words.

driggle	plondle	bozzle
ploble	chomdle	weggle
thumple	blattle	shrungle
priffle	muzle	flotle
stodle	slinkle	cheple
shubble	trinzle	strople
thofle	pudle	zingle
brentle	grunzle	blefle
fitle	shobble	chentle
flidle	bopple	shundle
plebble	trendle	kipple
thumple	blittle	biffle
spinkle	bleple	stozle
driggle	floble	bruple
chomple	trizle	frogle

Read the story "Todd's Best Moment" in Student Reader Six. Read each sentence below. Write <u>T</u> on the line if it is true and <u>F</u> if it is false. Use the Student Reader to check your answers.

<u>Todd's Best Moment</u>

1. Todd was not the best *football player* in the state.___

2. It was a gamble for Todd to run up the middle.___

3. An opponent landed on Todd just before he crossed the line.___

4. Todd's *team* lost the state title.___

5. The drizzle did not stop the game.___

_____
Rewrite the sentences, making them true. Underline or "scoop" syllables in the multisyllabic words.

1. _____

_____

2. _____

_____

3. _____

_____

4. _____

_____

5. _____

_____

Read the syllables on each side of the box. Draw a line to connect syllables to form real words.

bu	ple
dim	gle
gam	ble

trem	gle
hud	ble
jug	dle

mum	gle
shin	zle
nuz	ble

fa	ple
puz	ble
tem	zle

cat	ble
no	tle
jun	gle

muf	fle
fraz	dle
i	zle

Write the words above on the lines below. Read the words.

_____ _____ _____

_____ _____ _____

_____ _____ _____

_____ _____ _____

_____ _____ _____

Underline or "scoop" the syllables in each word. Find and circle all consonant-le exceptions.
Cross out the t and e to indicate the silent letters. e.g. whis(tle)

pestle	muddle	jostle
dabble	sickle	ramble
bugle	gobble	fumble
castle	mingle	bundle
staple	dabble	bustle
razzle	nestle	candle
muffle	hustle	table
gristle	apostle	thistle
jingle	dimple	trestle
rustle	puzzle	raffle
juggle	rifle	idle
thimble	sample	whistle
heckle	kindle	humble
unsettle	bristle	struggle
befuddle	subtitle	unstable

REVIEW- Mark the vowels in the words below.

scrub	__gle	fame
shame	think	shy
spring	pro	ill
pry	slave	hi
__tle	__ple	flake
prune	he	__dle
me	clap	crave
__fle	try	__zle
clothe	__ble	bring
stress	thump	shade

List the syllables above in the correct column below.

closed

_____

_____

_____

_____

_____

_____

_____

vowel-consonant-e

_____

_____

_____

_____

_____

_____

_____

open

_____

_____

_____

_____

_____

_____

consonant-le

_____

_____

_____

_____

_____

_____

Find the Syllable Exceptions:

closed: ild, old, olt, ost, ind   open: a and i
vowel-consonant-e: ive   consonant-le: stle

bustle	jolt	grind	wild
ago	have	host	whistle
Atlanta	instigate	give	across
blind	bold	olive	hustle
thistle	active	medicate	expensive
colt	nestle	gristle	castle
mild	captive	nestle	imitate
disruptive	impulsive	tundra	abode

Exceptions:

   closed   **vowel-consonant-e**

_____   _____

_____   _____

_____   _____

_____   _____

_____   _____

_____   _____

_____   _____

   open   **consonant-le**

_____   _____

_____   _____

_____   _____

_____   _____

_____   _____

_____   _____

_____   _____

Create sentences that include the vocabulary words below. Use a dictionary or electronic spell checker as needed. Underline or "scoop" each syllable in the vocabulary words.

6.1	**6.2**	**6.3**	**6.4**
abolishment	obstructed	constructively	idle
eventful	mulled	gratefully	tremble
novelty	billed	uselessly	fickle
development	abolished	restlessly	humble
consistently	bluffed	zestfully	resemble
profitable	refunded	regretfully	gobble
boldly	famished	trustfully	ramble
taxes	banished	respectfully	meddle
limitless	stressed	instinctively	mingle
lifeless	prolonged	effectively	huddle

Story Starter:
At the end of Step 6 create a story that includes many (at least 5) of the vocabulary words below. This story is about someone helping someone else. Underline each vocabulary word used from the list below.

kindly	finished	struggle	accomplishment
silently	wished	prideful	settle
dependable	respectful	distinctly	puzzle
expecting	strongest	longed	effectively
thankful	selflessly	hopefully	willingly